Japanese Cookbook

*Traditional Japanese Cuisine
in 80 Delectable Recipes
(2022 Guide for Beginners)*

Josh Andrus

Contents

Introduction

Each dish is dubbed "Gohan" by the Japanese. For example, breakfast is referred to as "asa-Gohan." A cup of boiling rice is also included in traditional Japanese meals, which can be served for supper, breakfast, or lunch. Okazu are side dishes that are served with broth and rice in Japan. While Japan is a small country, each of its regions and towns has its own distinct personality. Kanto (the large island's eastern portion) and Kansai foods are the most popular (the western section of the big island).

Kanto cuisine is known for its bold flavors, whereas Kansai cuisine is known for its delicate seasoning. In the Kansai and Kanto regions, many meals are prepared differently. Fried rice is a traditional Japanese dish that can be eaten for breakfast, lunch, or dinner.

Perfect arrangement, pure tastes, and unique dishes are characteristics of Japanese cuisine. Meals are historical and ceremonial events, with various main dishes served with boiled vegetables, pickles, and spice mixes – all presented in individually selected bowls. Japan's chain of hilly islands is crisscrossed by rivers, and it was from these abundant waterways that the Japanese obtained fresh fish, which is the highlight of most Japanese meals.

Japan has without a doubt established itself as one of the world's great culinary nations. New seasonal harvests and careful preparation are essential components of Japanese cuisine. Japanese cuisine has grown in popularity in recent years. It's no surprise that Japanese food is so popular, given its mastery of flavors and delicate balance of sweet and salty. Japanese and Japanese-inspired dishes, such as seafood and ramen, are available all over the world, including in local kitchens. Water is essential in Japanese cuisine, with dashi made from Kombu (kelp) and bonito particles suspended in water serving as the base for Japanese sauces. At the heart of Japanese cuisine are fresh, seasonal ingredients cooked simply in water. As a result, it is a good candidate for the "healthy" label.

The Japanese diet is built around the idea of long-term health.

Japanese food is not only delicious and appealing, but it also has a number of health benefits. Raw meats, added sweets or foods, and a lot of fruit and legumes are all part of traditional Japanese cuisine. Breast and cervical cancers, both of which are hormone-dependent, have historically been uncommon in Japan. This is due to a higher intake of vegetables, berries, healthy fats, high-fiber foods, and a lower total calorie intake. Japan has one of the lowest rates of heart disease development in the world, and it is even lower in developing countries. Because the Japanese diet is high in nutrients that promote heart health, heart disease is uncommon in Japan. Green tea is commonly served with Japanese meals and has a number of health benefits. Green tea has been shown to help with blood pressure reduction, immune system strengthening, and slowing the aging process. "Japanese Cookbook" provides a wide range of delectable Japanese dishes that incorporate these uncommon flavors. It is divided into six sections, each of which includes appetizers, snacks, breakfast, lunch, supper, desserts, and some of Japan's most famous dishes. Sushi and ramen dishes are also featured.

Read this book, prepare these dishes, and you'll have a delicious, tasty dinner every day.

Chapter 1
Traditional Japanese Breakfast Recipes

1.1 Pancakes with Japanese Red Beans

Time to cook: 45 minutes

Six servings Ingredients:

One teaspoon unflavored oil

1.1-pound red bean paste

1 tsp. baking powder

Two teaspoons water

2 Tbsp. honey

1 pound all-purpose flour

four large eggs

2/3 cup sugar

Method:

1. In a large mixing bowl, whisk the eggs, honey, and sugar until frothy.

2. 15 minutes of relaxation

3. Preheat a large nonstick frying pan over medium-low heat.

4. Spoon 3 Tablespoons batter into a spoon or a small quart container.

5. To keep it from drying out, place it in a dish and cover it with a wet cloth.

1.2 Japanese Skillet for Breakfast

1 hour of cooking time

Two servings Ingredients:

100g kale (curly)

2 to 4 eggs

Shiitake mushrooms (50g)

Grape tomatoes, 150g

150 grams sweet potatoes

12 medium onion

Two tablespoons of your preferred oil

The Dressing

One teaspoon turmeric powder

Dates: 1-2

Eight small cherry tomatoes

12 teaspoon black pepper

12 medium onion

Two teaspoons ginger

1 12 tbsp tomato ketchup

One teaspoon miso white

2 tbsp tahini (light)

Method:

1. Begin by combining all of the sauce's ingredients in a high-powered blender.

2. Heat one tablespoon of the oil in a heavy-bottomed pan.

3. Add the onion to the pan when it's medium-hot and cook for a few minutes before adding the butternut squash and mushrooms.

4. Cook, frequently stirring, until the potato softens, about 5 minutes.

5. In a small fry pan, heat the cooking oil and cook the eggs as desired.

Cooking Time: 30 minutes Serving Size: 2 Ingredients: 1.3 Japanese Vegetable Pancake

Two green onions

One tablespoon olive oil

120g fresh green cabbage

12 teaspoon ginger puree

Pinch of black pepper

One carrot, small

four eggs

One teaspoon soy sauce

80g unbleached flour

To Be Used

Spring onions, chopped

toasted sesame seeds

Salad cream or Sriracha mayonnaise

Method:

1. Whisk the eggs and wholemeal flour in a mixing bowl.

2. To make the pancake batter, combine all of the ingredients in a mixing bowl.

3. Stir in the cabbage, carrots, and spring onions, as well as the sesame oil, liquefied ginger, and plenty of black pepper.

4. To combine, thoroughly whisk everything together.

5. In a deep fryer, heat a small amount of oil and spoon in 14 of the bread dough.

6. Cook for a few minutes over medium-low heat until the bottom is light brown, then turn the pancakes gently with a spoon and continue to cook for a few minutes more until completely done.

1.4 Japanese Omelets Tamagoyaki

1 hour of cooking time

Ingredients: 1 serving size

a pinch of sea salt

As needed, use cooking oil.

One teaspoon mirin

One teaspoon sugar

One teaspoon soy sauce

four eggs

Method:

1. Begin by thoroughly whisking your whites in a mixing bowl.

2. Stir in 1 tablespoon sesame oil, mirin, and honey, as well as a pinch of salt.

3. Heat a small amount of cooking oil in a small saucepan over medium heat.

4. Pour a small amount of your egg mixture into the hot pan.

5. Using the kitchen roll, add more oil and a small amount of the egg mixture to the pan.

6. As you add egg and wrap it up each time, your egg sandwich will expand in size, making it easier to add additional layers.

7. Continue layering the egg until you've used it all up.

Sandwich with 1.5 Japanese Egg Omelet

Time to cook: 3 minutes

Two servings Ingredients:

One teaspoon Katsuobushi

2 tbsp. unsalted butter

Two white bread slices

Two tablespoons mayonnaise

three eggs

12 teaspoon of sugar

14 teaspoon of salt

Method:

1. Whisk together the eggs, salt, and sugar in a mixing bowl.

2. Spread one teaspoon of mayonnaise evenly on each piece of bread.

3. Spread Katsuobushi on a single piece of bread.

4. Preheat a microwaveable bowl over medium-high heat.

5. Add the butter and let it melt completely.

6. Pour in the egg mixture and continue to scramble it.

7. Carefully and softly place the combined eggs in the pan's corner.

8. Use a spatula if necessary.

9. Carefully remove the omelets from the pan and serve with katsuobushi-strewn bread.

1.6 Miso Mayo Japanese Omelets

Time to cook: 15 minutes

One serving Ingredients: 2 tablespoons mayonnaise

One avocado, small

Two scallions (green onions)

1 tsp white miso paste

One tablespoon soy sauce

2 to 3 eggs

Method:

1. Whisk together the eggs, cayenne pepper, half of the spring onion, and two tablespoons of liquid in a separate bowl.

2. Heat the oil in a large saucepan.

3. Drizzle in a little olive oil and stir it around to coat the bottom of the pan once it's hot.

4. Cook, constantly stirring, until the egg mixture is no longer runny.

5. While the eggs are frying, combine the miso powder and mayo and spread it over the bottom of the serving dish.

6. When the egg is just cooked and no longer runny, roll the omelet onto the dish on the upper edge of the miso mayonnaise.

1 Egg Tamagoyaki 1.7

1 hour of cooking time

Four servings Ingredients: 2 eggs

Brushing oils

12 tbsp sugar 14 cup water

14 teaspoon soy sauce 18 teaspoons salt

18 tspdashi powder

1. In a mixing bowl, combine the dashi, salt, sesame oil, sugar, and boiling water.

2. Combine all of the ingredients in a mixing bowl and stir until completely dissolved.

3. Whisk together the eggs and spice mix in a medium mixing bowl.

4. Combine all of the ingredients in a mixing bowl and thoroughly combine.

5. Heat a tamagoyaki pan over medium heat.

6. Apply a thin layer of oil to the pan.

7. Pour a quarter of the flour mixture into the pan and quickly swirl it around to cover it completely.

8. Once the egg has half-set, lightly rub it.

TamagoDashimaki 1.8

Time to cook: 15 minutes

Two servings Ingredients:

3 gm potato starch 34 tsp daikon

1 cup of dashi

1 tbsp. white soy sauce

14 cup eggs

Method:

1. Crack the eggs into a large mixing bowl.

2. In a separate bowl, combine the dashi, white sesame oil, and rice flour until the starch is completely dissolved.

3. Pour the dashi solution into the yolks and whisk vigorously to combine, trying to keep the bubbles to a minimum.

4. Preheat a 12-inch nonstick deep fryer over medium-high heat.

5. Pour in 14 of the flour mixture and allow to simmer.

6. Roll the dashimakiTamago towards the back of the pan, starting from the edge closest to you.

7. Place the dashimakitamago on a sushi mat and gently wrap it around the egg.

Hiroshima Okonomiyaki (1.9)

Time to cook: 50 minutes

Size of serving: 2

Ingredients:

One yakisoba noodle package

ONE EGG

1 tbsp chopped scallions

Four pork belly slices

14 cup bean sprout tempura (to taste)

Oil

cabbage (23 cups)

1 tsp. bonito powder

Batter Concoction

13 cups of water

One tablespoon mirin

12 cup all-purpose flour

Method:

1. Whisk the flour, milk, and mirin in a mixing bowl until smooth.

2. Spray a small amount of oil on a preheated electric skillet set to 350 degrees Fahrenheit.

3. Pour the mixture into the skillet with a spatula.

4. Completely cover the batter with lettuce, panko, black beans, and scallions.

5. Drizzle with a little oil and top with four pieces of pork belly.

6. Gently turn and push down the pancake with two okonomiyaki spoons.

7. Drizzle the okonomi sauce over the pasta and toss to evenly coat it.

1.10 Omelets with Japanese Pork Fried Rice

Time to cook: 30 minutes

Four servings Ingredients:

Black pepper and kosher salt

four large eggs

one scallion

To taste, cayenne pepper

14 cup okonomiyaki sauce 2 strips pork belly

Two cs of sushi rice

12 cup sliced yellow onion

a 12 cup cabbage

fourtbsp vegetable oil

Method:

1. Heat one tablespoon olive oil in a casserole dish over high heat until it begins to smoke.

2. Sauté half of the rice, tossing and flipping it halfway through.

3. Pour into a medium mixing bowl.

4. Return the skillet to high heat and cook until the oil begins to smoke.

5. Cook, turn, and occasionally toss for 3 minutes, or until the onion and carrots are soft and lightly browned in spots.

6. Cook, occasionally turning, until the pork is cooked through and lightly browned, about four minutes.

7. Prepare with okonomiyaki sauce.

After tossing in the scallions, season with chili, salt, and oil.

Chapter 2

Recipes for Traditional Japanese Lunches

2.1 Simple Tempura Batter

Time to cook: 10 minutes

Servings per recipe: 6

Ingredients:

1 cup unbleached all-purpose flour

13 cup ice-cold water

two egg whites

1. In a mixing bowl, whisk egg whites until foamy.

2. In a separate mixing bowl, whisk together the flour and ice water until just combined.

Cooking Time for Teriyaki Chicken: 15 minutes

Four servings Ingredients:

2 tsp corn starch

Green onions and sesame seeds

Two tablespoons ginger

Two garlic cloves

One teaspoon rice vinegar

14 tsp toasted sesame oil

2 Tbsp. honey

One teaspoon brown sugar

14 tbsp soy sauce

14 cups of water

One teaspoon olive oil

114-pound chicken breasts

1. Heat the olive oil in a 12-inch casserole dish over medium heat.

2. Cook for 3 - 4 minutes on top, then turn and cook for another 3 minutes, or until the center registers 160 degrees.

3. In a small bowl, whisk together the miso, water, sugar, brown sugar, garlic powder, soy sauce, garlic, onion, and starch while the chicken is cooking.

4. Stir the sauce into the chicken breast for 30 to 60 seconds or until the gravy has thickened.

5. While still warm, sprinkle with spring onions and red pepper flakes if desired.

2.3 Japanese-Inspired Salmon in a Single Pan

Time to cook: 40 minutes

Two servings Ingredients:

One tablespoon of coconut oil

One teaspoon kosher salt

1 pound sweet potato

1 tbsp toasted sesame seeds

One broccolini bunch

Two fillets of salmon

Marinade

2 tbsp toasted sesame seeds

One teaspoon honey

14 tbsp tamari sauce

12 tbsp Dijon mustard

1 tbsp sesame seed oil

1. Preheat the oven to 200 degrees Celsius.

2. Using a knife, cut the butternut squash into pieces.

3. Drizzle the rounds with coconut oil and arrange them on a baking sheet lined with parchment paper, leaving room for the shrimp and broccolini.

4. Stir in the spring onions and season with salt to taste.

5. Preheat the oven to 350 degrees Fahrenheit and bake for 25 minutes.

6. Meanwhile, in a mixing bowl, combine all of the leftover marinades.

7. Drizzle the marinade over the two fish fillets in the oven pan, which are surrounded by broccolini and butternut squash.

8. Preheat the oven to 350 degrees Fahrenheit and bake for 12-15 minutes.

2.4 Chicken Curry in Japan

Time to cook: 35 minutes

Size of each serving: 4

Ingredients:

To serve, pickled ginger

Japanese rice, steamed

Two green onions

1 tsp. sesame seeds

1 tbsp reduced-salt soy sauce

One teaspoon honey

Green beans (150g)

14 cup apple sauce (Coles)

1 Tbsp. vegetable oil

2 cup chicken broth

Two carrots, diagonally sliced

Two teaspoon curry powder

Two teaspoon tomato paste

600g thigh fillets of chicken

14 cup plain flour two garlic cloves

60g of butter

2cm fresh ginger piece

One medium brown onion

Method:

1. Heat the oil in a large deep cooking pot over a medium flame.

2. Cook for 5 minutes, or until the meat is evenly browned.

3. Transfer to a platter to cool.

4. Melt the butter in the same pan over low heat.

5. In a mixing bowl, combine the fish sauce and tomato sauce.

6. Pour in one-fourth cup of water and the rest of the stock.

7. Bring to a low boil, then turn off the heat.

8. Add the chicken and carrots and toss to combine.

9. Cook for another 5 minutes, or until the beans are tender.

Spring cabbage and green onions can be added to the dish at the last minute.

Donburi Teriyaki Beef 2.5

Time to cook: 20 minutes

Four servings Ingredients:

1 tsp. sesame seeds

One red chili, long

a single carrot

Two sliced green onions

12 cup liquid chicken stock

four eggs

Two cloves garlic

2cm ginger piece

1/12 cup white rice

12 cup teriyaki sauce

One onion, red

Two teaspoons vegetable oil

500g rump steak (beef)

12 cup thawed frozen peas

Method:

1. Heat the oil in a large deep cooking pot over a medium flame.

2. Cook for 5 minutes, or until the meat is evenly browned.

3. Set it aside to cool.

4. Melt the butter in the same pan over low heat.

5. Brown the onions in a skillet over medium heat.

6. Cook, occasionally stirring, for three minutes, or until golden brown.

7. Cook for a minute after adding the ginger and garlic.

In a mixing bowl, combine the fish sauce and tomato sauce.

9. Pour in one-fourth cup of water and the rest of the stock.

10. Bring to a low boil, then turn off the heat.

11. Add the chicken and carrots and toss to combine.

12. Cook for another 5 minutes, or until the beans are tender.

13. You can add spring cabbage and green onions to the dish.

Spicy Miso Chicken Wings with Japanese Potato Salad (2.6 oz.)

Time to cook: 30 minutes

Four servings Ingredients:

to taste, black pepper

Eight thighs of chicken

Two teaspoons honey

One teaspoon rice vinegar

12 cup white miso soup

Four tablespoons melted butter

Method:

1. Preheat the oven to 425 degrees F.

2. In a large mixing bowl, combine the butter, soy sauce, sugar, rice vinegar, and garlic powder and thoroughly mix with a spoon or spoon.

3. In the bowl, rub the miso-butter mixture all over the chicken.

4. Arrange the pan in a thin layer in a baking dish and bake for 30 minutes.

5. Bake for 30 to 40 minutes, depending on the size of your oven. Once or twice, turn the chicken breasts over. When it turns lightly golden and crisp on the outside and 160 to 165 degrees on the inside, it is done.

Japanese Fried Chicken (2.7)

Time to cook: 45 minutes

Size of each serving: 4

Ingredients:

12 tsp black pepper

For serving, a wedge of lemon

1 cup starch from potatoes

14 teaspoon of sea salt

Four chicken thighs, skin on

Oil from peanuts

3 tbsp of soy sauce

Two tablespoons sugar

2 tsp. smashed garlic

2 tbsp of dry sake

1/12 teaspoon ginger

Method:

1. In a deep cake pan large enough to hold the chicken, combine the ginger, cloves, wine, soy sauce, and sugar.

2. Brush the marinade over the chicken pieces.

3. Refrigerate it for 12 to 24 hours after covering it.

4. Brush off any excess potato starch before frying each piece of chicken.

5. Fry three or four slices at a time, keeping the oil temperature at 325°F.

6. Garnish with a lemon slice, lettuce, and whipped cream for a cold, refreshing contrast, as well as a lemon wedge if desired.

Tasmanian Smoked Salmon Rolls and Dip (2.8 oz.)

Time to cook: 10 minutes

13 servings Ingredients:

12 cup chopped fresh chives

One ripe avocado

2 tbsp chopped fresh dill

One tablespoon mint, fresh

One celery stick bunch

200g salad leaves, mixed

Cream cheese (250g)

smoked salmon (500g)

1. Wrap the bamboo mat with cotton wool and store it.

2. Arrange three pieces of smoked salmon on a bamboo skewer, overlapping them to form a rectangle.

3. In a mixing bowl, combine the sour cream, mint, dill, and onions.

4. Spoon a few teaspoons of the solution onto the center section of the smoky salmon.

5. Finish with a celery stick and wrap it in the bamboo mat as if it were sushi.

Zaru Soba (2.9)

Time to cook: 15 minutes

Two servings Ingredients:

Two soba noodle bunches

Sauce for dipping

Soy sauce (50ml)

Mirin (50ml)

dashi stock (200ml)

Method:

1. Combine the dipping sauce ingredients in a saucepan and heat over medium heat.

2. Cook for about 15 seconds, or until tiny bubbles appear around the edge, before turning off the heat.

3. Allow for solidification at room temperature.

4. Shake the colander vigorously to remove any water from the bottom, then set aside until needed.

5. Serve soba noodles in a large dish for sharing or on two plates for individual servings.

2.10 Yakitori Chicken Thighs

Time to cook: 15 minutes

Six servings Ingredients:

12 tsp ginger Scallions

1 pound of chicken liver

One teaspoon brown sugar

Two cloves garlic

14 tbspmirin

Two teaspoons sake

12 cup soy sauce (dark)

1. Put the chicken in a small bowl and cut it into 1-inch chunks.

2. In a small pot, combine soy sauce or soy, miso, sake or wine, black pepper, garlic, and onion.

3. Bring to a low boil, then reduce to low heat and continue to cook for 10 minutes, or until the sauce thickens.

4. Skewer the chicken parts and cook or broil for three minutes for the organs, ten minutes for the gizzards, and five minutes for the thighs, rotating halfway through.

2.11 Crispy Miso Pork Belly with Hot Soba in Broth

Time to cook: 50 minutes

Servings per recipe: 6

Ingredients:

Soba noodles (270g)

Eggs, soft-boiled

Three shallots, long and green

4 cup chicken broth

Two cloves garlic

3cm ginger piece

205g miso paste white

34 cup mirin

14 cup virgin olive oil

Brown sugar (150g)

1 pound boneless pork belly

Method:

1. Arrange the pulled pork on a tray and cut the flesh into 1cm slices with a sharp knife.

2. Preheat the oven to 150° Celsius.

3. Cook for 2 1/2 hours or until the meat is tender.

4. Combine the sugar, 100g soybeans, and mirin in a separate dish.

5. Continue to cook for another fifteen minutes or until the apples are lightly caramelized.

6. Remove from the oven and set aside to cool for 15 minutes.

7. In a medium skillet over moderately low heat, heat the remaining two tablespoons of oil to make the miso broth foundation.

8. Cook, occasionally stirring, for 2-3 minutes, or until the garlic, ginger, and shallot are soft and aromatic.

2.12 Caramelized Carrots with Tonkatsu Chicken

Time to cook: 35 minutes

Ten servings Ingredients:

30 grams salted butter

Two lemons, cut in half 4 x 200g chicken breasts

Grapeseed oil (75ml)

2 tbsp Chinese chili paste

Panko breadcrumbs (65g)

two large eggs

70g unbleached flour

Carrots Caramelized

carrots (450g)

90 grams salted butter

Method:

1. In a small saucepan, heat 30g oil for the caramelized carrots.

2. Combine the carrots and one tablespoon of water in a mixing bowl.

3. Simmer for ten minutes, or until the butter has melted, the water has evaporated, and the bottom carrots have turned golden brown.

4. Preheat the oven to 100° Celsius.

5. Sift the flour into a large, shallow basin. Whisk together the eggs and chili paste in a small bowl.

6. Coat each roast chicken in the following order: flour, egg, and panko crumbs.

7. Cook for 3-4 minutes, or until the bottom of the chicken is browned.

8. Cook for another 3-4 minutes on the other side, or until it is caramelized.

2.13 Tsukune (Japanese Chicken Meatballs) 35-minute cooking time

Eight servings Ingredients:

12 teaspoon cornflour 12 teaspoons sake

One teaspoon fresh ginger juice

One teaspoon soy sauce (light)

ONE EGG

One tablespoon onion, grated

50 g of chicken fat

12 tsp salt 450 g chicken breast

Sauce

Mirin (40ml)

12 teaspoon sugar

Soy sauce (40ml)

Method:

1. Bring all of the Sauce ingredients to a boil in a saucepan.

2. Reduce the heat to low or medium-low and cook for another 4-5 minutes.

3. Combine the poultry mince, chicken stock, and salt in a mixing bowl.

4. Thoroughly combine until the meat mince becomes sticky.

5. Toss in the remaining ingredients and thoroughly mix.

6. Scoop up the meatball with a spoon and place it in the saucepan.

7. Cook the meatball for 5 minutes or until fully cooked.

8. Take the meatballs out of the pan and serve.

Recipes for Traditional Japanese Dinners, Chapter 3

3.1 FiorettoCauli Blossom and Wok-Fried Broccolini

Time to cook: 40 minutes

Size of each serving: 13

Ingredients:

To make the Tsukune Meatballs

1 to 2 tablespoons olive oil

One teaspoon avocado oil

0.5 cup ginger

One shallot, 0.8 oz

1 pound of ground chicken breast

1 Tbsp. coconut aminos

One large yolk of an egg

12 tsp coarse sea salt 14 tsp white pepper

Two scallions bulbs

One teaspoon sesame oil, toasted

Regarding the Sauce and Serving

One butter lettuce head

14 cup teriyaki sauce (Keto)

1. Combine the components from the chicken and the egg yolk in a water-filled dish.

2. Grate the ginger and squeeze the liquid into a dish.

3. Line a sheet pan with parchment paper.

4. Using a cookie scoop, form 13 meatballs and place them on a baking sheet.

5. Form the meatballs into tiny patties.

6. On the first half, pan fry them in coconut oil for about 2.5 minutes over medium heat.

7. Serve with buttered lettuce and a thin layer of teriyaki sauce on top.

3.2 Crusted Black Sesame Salmon with Wasabi Slaw and Edamame

Time to cook: 10 minutes

Four servings Ingredients: lime juice from 2 lemons

12 tsp sesame oil

12 cup mayonnaise (Kewpie)

2 tsp. wasabi paste

Two green onions

edamame beans, 12 cups shelled

Four fillets of salmon

12 Lombok cucumber 12 continental cucumber

4 tbsp sesame seeds, black

Method:

1. Remove the skin from the fish fillets, spread sesame seeds on a plate, and coat one side of the fish with the seeds.

2. Cook the fish sesame seed side down in a heavy-bottomed pan with a little oil over medium heat.

3. Combine the wombok, cucumbers, soybean beans, red onion, and chill in a mixing bowl.

4. Combine the mayonnaise, wasabi powder, soy sauce, and lemon juice in a mixing bowl, then taste and adjust the seasoning to taste.

5. Combine the salad and the dressing in a large mixing bowl.

6. Arrange the fish fillets on top of the slaw with a slice of lime.

Cooking Time for Marmite Chicken: 30 minutes

Two servings Ingredients:

One beaten egg white

a few cooking oils

14 teaspoon baking soda 60g cornstarch

350g thigh of chicken

To make the Marmite Sauce

1.5 teaspoon maltose

1 tbsp sesame oil

2 tsp. light soy sauce

1.5 teaspoon honey

Two tablespoons Marmite

45ml (three tablespoons) water

To make the Chicken Marinade

1 tbsp rice wine

1 tbsp vegetable oil

14 tsp white pepper

2 tsp corn starch

One teaspoon soy sauce (light)

Method:

1. Marinate the precooked meat for thirty minutes.

2. In a mixing bowl, combine the flour and baking powder.

3. Coat the seasoned chicken in the arrowroot powder soda mixture, then in the egg white.

4. Deep-fry the chicken until it is golden brown.

5. Take the pan off the heat and pat it dry with a towel.

6. Heat all of the sauce ingredients in a skillet until they form a thick gravy.

7. Coat the chicken in the gravy.

3.4 Curry with Japanese Chicken, Broccoli, and Mushrooms

Time to cook: 30 minutes

Two servings Ingredients:

The soy sauce

To serve, steamed rice

1 tbsp. white miso paste

300ml chicken broth

Ginger is about the size of a thumb.

One tablespoon curry powder, mild

Four green onions

Garlic 1 garlic clove

Broccoli, 150g

300g thigh fillets of chicken

button mushrooms (100g)

twotbsp groundnut oil

Method:

1. Cover the cauliflower in a dish with boiling water and set it aside for 5 minutes.

2. Next, in a nonstick skillet, heat one tablespoon olive oil and brown the chicken for 2 to 3 minutes, or until browned.

3. Cook for 2-3 minutes, or until the button mushrooms are brown, then remove.

4. Stir in the remaining tablespoon of olive oil, along with the green onions, garlic, and pepper.

5. Return the meat and vegetables to the pan for another 2-3 minutes of cooking.

6. After adding the curry powder, cook for a minute.

7. In a mixing bowl, combine the miso and water.

8. Bring to a boil, then reduce to low heat and continue to cook for 15 minutes on medium-high heat.

Whole Chicken Shoyu Ramen 3.5

Time to cook: 5 hours

Five servings Ingredients:

1 Tbsp. vegetable oil

The stock of 2.5kg whole chicken

Two grated ginger

Two shiitake mushrooms, dried

One garlic clove

a single carrot

20cm kombu piece

Six green onions

a couple of handfuls of bonito flakes

Crispy Crispy Chicken

twotbsp vegetable oil

ginger, finely chopped

Two garlic cloves

100g miso white

Eggs Marinated in Soy

two eggs

Mirin (50ml)

One teaspoon caster sugar

Soy sauce (100ml)

Method:

1. Cool the chicken in the marinade for at least 5 minutes, turning it occasionally.

2. Preheat the oven to 200° Celsius.

3. Take the chicken's legs off (drumsticks).

4. Roast for 1 hour, rotating halfway until everything is caramelized.

5. For the last thirty minutes, crisp the skins in the microwave.

6. Remove the chicken breasts and onion rings from the oven and set them aside to cool.

7. Add the remaining stock ingredients to the pan with the dashi, then lower the main body into it. Simmer the water on low heat for 2 12 hours.

Meanwhile, in a skillet, heat the sunflower oil and add the chopped thighs and drumstick flesh for the crispy chicken.

9. Cook for 5 minutes, tossing once in a while.

Tataki (Seared Tuna) 3.6

Time to cook: 7 minutes

Four servings Ingredients:

tbsp sprouts

2 tbsp. sliced red chili

One tablespoon of vegetable oil

1 tbsp toasted sesame seeds

12 oz. tuna block

Dressing for Tuna Tataki

One teaspoon ginger, grated

One onion (spring)

One teaspoon lime juice

1 tbsp sesame oil

Two teaspoons soy sauce

1. Combine all of the ingredients for the Tataki sauce in a small dish and set aside.

2. Heat a small amount of oil in a nonstick pan over high heat.

3. On a clean board or platter, season the tuna liberally with sea salt and black pepper.

4. Cook the fish for 15-20 seconds at a time, being careful not to overcook it.

5. Transfer the fried tuna to a clean cutting board and set it aside for 5 minutes.

6. Place it on your casserole plate after thinly slicing it against the grain.

Miso Mackerel with Chili Brown Rice 3.7

Time to cook: 20 minutes

Two servings Ingredients:

One red pepper

Two green onions

Brown rice, 150g

1cm ginger piece

2 tsp caster sugar (golden)

Two tablespoons mirin

Two mackerel (whole)

4 tbsp. white miso oil

Method:

1. Oil the fish and place it skin-side up on the pan.

2. Using a pastry brush, brush the vinegar, sugar, and mirin mixture all over the meat.

3. Prepare the rice.

4. Combine the ginger, jalapeno, and spring onion in a small jug with a little oil.

5. Preheat the grill to high heat and cook the mackerel for 5 minutes.

6th. Serve with rice.

Tsukune with Japanese-style Quinoa 3.8

Time to cook: 40 minutes

Size of each serving: 4

Ingredients:

One tangerine

2 Tbsp. honey

5 tbspmirin 4 tbsp soy sauce

a small bunch of coriander Sesame oil to serve

frying oil

200g quinoa (mixed red and black)

Two teaspoons grated ginger to make

4 tbsp. panko breadcrumbs

One clove garlic

Two green onions

450g minced chicken

1. To make the glaze, combine all of the ingredients and set aside four tablespoons for the quinoa.

2. Using your hands, combine the mince, garlic, green onions, ginger, and breadcrumbs in a mixing bowl.

3. Season to taste, then form the ingredients into tiny meatballs, about two teaspoons each.

4. Skewer each stick three times.

5. Heat a little oil in a large nonstick roasting pan.

6. Before serving, toss the wet, cooked quinoa with the conserved glaze and coriander.

7. To serve, arrange a few skewers on each plate and top with toasted quinoa.

3.9 Soba Noodles with Sake-Poached Chicken

Time to cook: 40 minutes

Four servings Ingredients:

Enoki mushroom (150g)

One red chili, long

One bunch bokchoy 270g soba noodle packet

2 cups liquid chicken stock

Two chicken breast fillets (180g)

14 cup soy sauce (light)

1 tsp caster sugar

12 cup shochu

20g shiitake mushrooms, dried

1. Soak the shiitake in a heatproof dish with two cups of boiling water.

2. Set aside for 5 minutes before draining and reserving the mushroom juice.

3. Bring the sake, sesame oil, sugar, coconut milk, and saved mushroom juice to a low boil in a saucepan, stirring occasionally.

4. Reduce the heat to low and cook the meat for ten minutes.

5. Add the noodles, enoki, and shiitake mushrooms and toss to combine.

6. Cook for ten minutes or until the noodles are tender.

3.10 Soup with Japanese Pumpkin and Tofu

Time to cook: 25 minutes

Four servings Ingredients:

75g spinach leaves, baby

200g mushrooms, mixed

Two teaspoons mirin

100g firm silken tofu

1 pound butternut pumpkin

14 tbsp soy sauce

Two teaspoons dashi stock powder

1. Heat lightly boiling water in a large skillet over medium heat.

2. Bring to a boil, then reduce to low heat and cook for 10 to 15 minutes, or until the pumpkins are tender but not mushy.

3. In a mixing bowl, combine the dashi powders, sesame oil, and miso.

4. Simmer for 5 minutes or until the tofu is thoroughly warmed.

5. Cook for 30 seconds or until the fresh basil and mushrooms wilt.

6. Remove from the heat.

7. Spoon the soup into hot serving dishes to serve.

3.11 Miso Butter-Slathered Ocean Trout

1 hour of cooking time

Size of each serving: 4

Ingredients:

One red chili, long

2cm ginger piece

One tablespoon honey

Four fillets of ocean trout

Eight green onions

zest, finely grated

One lemon, squeezed

80g of butter

12 tbsp. soy sauce

1 tbsp. white miso paste

Method:

1. Preheat the oven to 220° Celsius.

2. Place the spring onions in a heatproof dish, cover with boiling water, and set aside for two minutes to soften.

3. Drain and set aside the water.

4. In a mixing bowl, combine the butter, miso, sesame oil, lime juice and zest, and honey.

5. Arrange two loosely curled green onions in the center of the paper.

6. Apply the butter mixture to each piece of fish with a pastry brush.

7. Remove the packages from the oven and allow them to cool for 2 minutes before unwrapping.

3.12 Japanese Garage Chicken
Time to Cook: 20 minutes

Four servings Ingredients:

Chicken thigh fillets (800g)

100 g potato flour or cornstarch

4cm ginger piece

1 tsp. caster sugar

One tablespoon sake (cooking)

Two teaspoons soy sauce

Bok Choy with Soy Sauce

One bunch young bokchoy

Two teaspoons soy sauce

1 Tbsp. vegetable oil

Method:

1. Combine the chicken stock, sake, onion, and sugar in a glass or ceramic dish.

2. Toss in the meat to coat it with the sauce.

3. Cover and place in the refrigerator for 1 hour to marinate.

4. Preheat the oven to 200° Celsius.

5. Bake for six minutes, or until brown and tender, rotating halfway through.

6. Meanwhile, in a large frypan over medium-low heat, heat the oil for the soy-fried bokchoy.

7. Place the bokchoy in the pan, cut side down.

8. Cook for 1-2 minutes, covered, or until just cooked.

9. Arrange the rice in individual serving dishes and serve.

10. Sprinkle with scallions and chicken.

3.13 Pickled Vegetables with Teriyaki Salmon

1 hour of cooking time

Size of each serving: 4

Ingredients:

Rice, steamed

One teaspoon sesame seeds, black

One teaspoon sake

Four fillets of skinless salmon

One teaspoon caster sugar

14 cup tamari two tablespoons mirin Pickled Vegetables

12 daikon radishes

2 tbsp drained pickled ginger

1 tsp. caster sugar

One carrot, small

Rice vinegar, 100ml

1 pound Lebanese cucumber

Method:

1. In a small mixing bowl, combine the soy sauce, honey, miso, and sweet rice, stirring to combine.

2. Place the fish in a small bowl, pour over the miso mixture, and refrigerate for 20 to 30 minutes.

3. In the meantime, place the cucumber in a strainer over the sink for the pickled vegetables.

4. After adding two tablespoons of salt, set aside for ten minutes. On high heat for 5 minutes.

5. Allow cooling slightly before adding the cucumber, carrot, daikon, and ginger.

6. Chill while you wait for the salmon to cook.

Recipes for Japanese Snacks, Salads, and Desserts

Salad with Soba Noodles

Time to cook: 25 minutes

Size of serving: 8

Ingredients:

In order to make the Spicy Peanut Sauce

14 cup hot sauce

12 cup roasted peanuts

One lime juice

One garlic clove

2 tbsp sesame seed oil

Two teaspoons honey

Five teaspoons water

5 tbsp of soy sauce

5 tbsp peanut butter

To make the Salad

four cups purple cabbage

10 oz. soba noodles

One small red bell pepper

1 pound chicken breast

Method:

1. Puree the sauce ingredients in a large mixing bowl. Add the peanuts and mix well.

2. Cook the meat in a pan over medium heat. Season with salt and pepper to taste.

3. Chop the red peppers, lettuce, and coriander to your desired size for the salad.

4. Cook the noodles according to the package directions.

5. Toss everything together in a large mixing bowl with just enough dressing to coat everything evenly.

Salad with Teriyaki Chicken and Grilled Pineapple

Time to cook: 15 minutes

Two servings Ingredients:

Two small avocados

2 tbsp sesame seeds

12 cup cooked quinoa

12 large cherry tomatoes

12 small pineapple

One head of baby cos lettuce

Three teaspoons tamari sauce

1 tsp. sesame seeds

Two breasts of chicken

One tablespoon honey

Method:

1. In a large mixing bowl, combine all of the tamari, sugar, and one teaspoon of sesame oil.

2. Gently fold in the chicken breasts.

3. Sauté the pineapple pieces for a few minutes on high in a large frying pan or grilling pan.

4. Lower the heat to medium-high and cook the chicken for 5-6 minutes on each side.

5. Cut the chicken into pieces and toss with the greens in sesame oil.

Panna Cotta with Strawberries, White Chocolate, and Matcha

Time to cook: 20 minutes

Four servings Ingredients:

1 tsp powdered green tea

One teaspoon caster sugar

300g full-fat milk

Two teaspoons powdered gelatin

White chocolate (65g)

300g cream, thickened

150g strawberries, fresh

Method:

1. In a small saucepan, combine the cream, Mocha powder, icing sugar, gelatin, and chocolate mousse.

2. Quickly pour the milk into the pot.

3. Strain the panna cotta liquid into a pouring pitcher, then pour it into the prepared panna cotta pans.

4. Refrigerate your tin for at least four hours to allow it to set.

Celeriac KatsuSando 4.4

Time to cook: 35 minutes

Four servings Ingredients:

100g panko breadcrumbs vegetable frying oil

50g unbleached flour

One egg, one tablespoon olive oil, a light drizzle

One celeriac, large

To Be Used

Eight white bread slices

4 tbsptonkatsu sauce

One teaspoon rice vinegar

celeriac trimmings

2 to 3 tablespoons buttermilk

Method:

1. Preheat the oven to 190 degrees F and line a grill rack with parchment paper.

2. Bake the celeriac pieces in the oven for 20-25 minutes.

3. Combine the flavored flour, egg mixture, and panko breadcrumbs in three shallow bowls.

4. Toss the celeriac pieces in the wheat first, then in the egg mixture, and finally in the breadcrumbs until well coated.

5. To make a quick remoulade, combine the buttermilk, vinegar, and grated celeriac in a mixing bowl with a pinch of salt.

6. After frying for 1-2 minutes on each side, drain on kitchen paper until crispy and brown.

Yakitori Chicken Skewers with Miso 4.5

Time to cook: 20 minutes

Size of serving: 2

Ingredients:

250g thigh fillets of chicken

Three thick spring onions

2 tbsp sugar, 4 tbspmirin

Four teaspoon miso paste

1. Soak the wood skewer in freshwater for fifteen minutes.

2. Combine the vinegar, sugars, and mirin in a mixing bowl and whisk until the sugar is completely dissolved.

3. Alternately thread the meat and scallions onto skewers.

4. Brush the skewers with some of the sauce, then grill until done, brushing with more sauce as needed.

4.6 Tosazu Dressed Grilled Little Gem Lettuce

Time to cook: 15 minutes

Four servings Ingredients:

To serve, two tablespoons rapeseed oil toasted sesame seeds

Four tiny gem lettuces

Dressing

1/12 teaspoon mirin

katsuobushi 2g

One teaspoon caster sugar

12 tsp. soy sauce

Four teaspoon rice vinegar

Method:

1. In a small saucepan, whisk together the vinegar, honey, soy sauce, mirin, and a pinch of salt to make the dressing.

2. Top with the katsuobushi.

3. Toss the salad quarters with the cane sugar and a pinch of salt and pepper in a mixing bowl.

4. Cook the romaine, cut-side up, over a hot BBQ or grill grate for 1-2 minutes per side, in groups if necessary, until thoroughly charred.

5. Arrange the pieces on a plate and drizzle with some of the dressing before finishing with the toasted pine nuts.

Sake Martini (4.7)

Time to cook: 3 minutes

One serving size

Ingredients: 12 oz. sake

Sliced cucumber

2 12 oz. gin

Method: 1. Gather all of the necessary materials.

2. Pour the gin or alcohol and sake into an ice-filled mixing glass.

3. Combine everything thoroughly.

4. Strain into a chilled martini glass halfway full of ice.

5. Garnish with a cucumber slice or a green olive.

Grilled Corn Salad with Parmesan and Miso Ponzu (4.8 stars)

1 hour of cooking time

Size of each serving: 4

Ingredients:

14 cup parmesan two witlof

Oil from vegetables

TogarashiShichimi

Five cobs of sweet corn

Ponzu Miso

12 tbsp. rice wine vinegar

a teaspoon of lemon juice

Two tablespoons miso white

12 teaspoon soy sauce

Kewpie mayonnaise (100g)

Method:

1. Combine all of the ingredients for the balsamic ponzu in a mixing bowl and stir to combine.

2. Preheat a chargrill pan or a lightly oiled grill pan to high heat.

3. Grill four corn cobs for 5-6 minutes, flipping every now and then.

4. Preheat the oven to 180°C and fill a large pot halfway with olive oil.

5. Fry the kernels for 4-5 minutes, occasionally stirring, until they are brown and crisp.

6. To serve, arrange the leftover fried potatoes and parmesan on a large plate or bowl.

4.9 Miso Caramel Madeleines

Time to cook: 50 minutes

12 servings Ingredients: 2 tablespoons almond meal

three egg whites

100g icing sugar, pure

2 tbsp. regular flour

1 tsp. runny honey

100g butter (unsalted)

Caramel Miso

175-gram caramel

30g miso white

180ml of pure cream

Method:

1. Combine all of the miso caramel ingredients in a medium saucepan over medium heat.

2. Heat the oil and sugar in a small saucepan over medium heat, stirring constantly.

3. In a large mixing bowl, whisk together the icing sugar, wheat flour, and almond flour.

4. Preheat the oven to 180° Celsius.

5. preheat oven to 350°F and bake for 12-14 minutes, or until the center springs back when pressed.

Miso Butter Snapper with Broccolini 4.10

Time to cook: 20 minutes

Two servings Ingredients:

12 lime juice

Spring onion, thinly sliced

150g mushrooms, mixed

1 tsp. sesame seeds

One teaspoon of peanut oil

Two red chilies, small

One teaspoon soy sauce

Two snapper fillets, 180g

1 tbsp sesame oil

Two broccolini bunches

25g unsalted softened butter

One teaspoon miso paste

Method:

1. Preheat the oven to 200° Celsius. Line a cookie sheet with baking paper.

2. Miso and butter are combined and smeared on top of the snapper.

3. Combine lime juice, pepper, soy sauce, and rice flour in a mixing bowl.

4. Toss in the gnocchi, onions, and green onions, and distribute evenly in the baking dish.

5. Roast for 18–20 seconds, or until the fish is cooked through and the broccolini is tender.

4.11 Miso Grilled Fish with Snow Pea Salad

Time to cook: 2 hours

Four servings Ingredients:

2 tbsp sesame seed oil

2 tbsp sesame seeds

2 tbspmirin and 2 tbsp rice vinegar

Snow peas (200g)

1 pound Lebanese cucumber

Noodles Udon

Salad with snow peas

a third of a cup of red miso paste

600g fillets of fish

One teaspoon soy sauce

2 tsp. caster sugar

34 cup mirin

Method:

1. In a small saucepan, combine the soy, mirin, and honey and bring to a simmer over medium heat.

2. Gently whisk in the miso until completely smooth.

3. Add the fish to the pan and toss to coat when it's cool enough to handle.

4. Cover with plastic wrap and place in the refrigerator for at least two hours or overnight.

5. Preheat the grill to medium-high. Cover a wire rack with foil.

6. Remove the fish from the marinade and grill it for 5 minutes, or until brown and caramelized.

7. In the meantime, season the salad ingredients and combine them in a bowl.

Teriyaki Fish Parcels (4.12 oz.)

Time to cook: 45 minutes

Size of each serving: 4

Ingredients:

a third cup of bean sprouts

Serve with coriander leaves.

Shiitake mushrooms (200g)

200g podded frozen edamame

2 tspmirin

4cm ginger piece

4 x 150g fillets of ling fish

14 cup soy sauce (dark)

a teaspoon of honey

Two tablespoons of sake

1. Combine the miso, rice, soy sauce, sugar, and ginger; pour over the salmon and marinate for 30 minutes.

2. Preheat the grill or the oven to 225°F.

3. Arrange a piece of fish in the center of each dish, top with mushrooms, and drizzle with one tablespoon of the leftover marinade.

4. Place it on a grill and cover the lid, or bake it in the oven for fifteen minutes or until heated through.

5. In the meantime, place the edamame in a dish, cover it with boiling water, and set it aside for five minutes to soak.

Recipes for Japanese Sushi, Sashimi, Ramen, and Bento

5.1 Summer Fruit Sushi

Time to cook: 40 minutes

Ten servings Ingredients:

Coconut, toasted

Candy cane crushed

sliced nuts

chocolate shavings

1 tbsp desiccated coconut

Summer fruit assortment

12 c. coconut milk

2 – 3 tbsp light condensed milk

1 pound sushi rice

Method:

1. Rinse the rice in a strainer under running water until it is clean.

2. Place the grains in a pan.

3. Use coconut milk and whipped cream to adjust the richness to your liking.

4. Gently fold in the desiccated almonds, then transfer to a glass bowl.

5. Place the wrapped sushi in the refrigerator for 30 minutes to cool.

5.2 Sushi Fried Rice in 5 Minutes or Less

Time to cook: 15 minutes

Size of each serving: 4

Ingredients:

One sheet nori

1 tbsp. toasted sesame seeds

14 cup ginger 14 avocado slices

four green onions

425g tuna in a can

1 Tbsp. vegetable oil

Two packets of 250g rice that is black

300g corn kernels from a can

Green beans (150g)

Dressing with Soy Sauce and Wasabi

1 tbsp sesame oil

One tablespoon wasabi paste

2 Tbsp. rice wine vinegar

2 tsp. caster sugar

Two teaspoons soy sauce

Method:

1. To make the soy and horseradish dressing, combine all of the ingredients in a jug and whisk until the sugar is completely dissolved.

2. Preheat a skillet over medium heat. Fill the container halfway with oil.

3. Swirl it around to coat.

4. Cook the beans in a skillet for two minutes, or until the vegetables are soft.

5. In a mixing bowl, combine the rice, maize, half of the onions, and half of the sauce.

6. Continue to stir-fry for three minutes or until thoroughly heated.

7. Divide the rice mixture among individual serving dishes and serve.

5.3 Ramen Noodles with Japanese Lamb Miso

Time to cook: 15 minutes

Size of each serving: 4

Ingredients:

Four green onions

Two red chilies, long

2 c. Hokkien noodle

Two teaspoons soy sauce

a single carrot

200g brown Swiss mushrooms

Lamb leg steaks (600g)

1 tsp. sunflower oil

Green beans, 150 g

Two teaspoon miso paste

Method:

1. Brush half of the miso paste over the steaks, then chargrill for 5–8 minutes per side on a lightly floured chargrill pan.

2. Rest for 5 minutes before slicing.

3. Heat the oil in a wok and stir-fry the beans, carrots, and mushrooms until lightly browned.

4. Cook for 4-5 minutes, or until the vinegar, two tablespoons of water, vermicelli, and soy are just tender.

5. Arrange the noodles, vegetables, and soup in separate bowls.

5.4 Ramen Noodles in a Jar on the Go Cooking Time: 10 minutes

Four servings Ingredients:

One sheet dry seaweed 1 cup firm tofu

two eggs

1 pound carrots

2 quarts sugar snap peas

One ramen noodle packet new Ramen Soup Base

2 cups piping hot water

2 tbsp. white miso paste

2 cups chicken-flavored liquid stock

Method:

1. Hard boil the eggs and cut them in half.

2. Layer fresh noodles on top of the miso paste in a container.

3. Place a full cup of Massel fluid chicken broth in a jar.

4. Add another half cup of lukewarm water to the jar.

5. Arrange julienned sweet snap peas, onions, cubed tofu, and a half egg on top of the pot noodles.

6. Cover the jar with a lid and set it aside for 5-6 minutes.

Shoko Premium Bento Lunchbox 5.5

1 hour of cooking time

One serving size

Ingredients: Kuri Japanese chestnuts, mashed

Aubergine pickled

Salad with pasta

Tempura vegetables

Tamagoyaki

Method:

1. Arrange the prepared items in a bento box.

2. Serve right away.

Sushi Rice Hand Rolls (5.6)

Time to cook: 10 minutes

Size of serving: 8

Ingredients: green sprouts

mayonnaise with shiso

Lettuce \sKaiware

One nori pack

Tuna, ikura, and salmon

1 pound sushi rice

Method:

1. Place a nori sheet next to you, a thick side up, and a large scoop of rice noodles on the lower side.

2. Temaki Sushi is made by sprinkling rice on the thick side of nori.

3. Cover half of the nori with a triangle of rice.

4. Arrange the filling ingredients on top of the rice, with the majority of the filling on top.

5. To make a cone, roll the top left edge up to the center of the nori's top border.

Sushi Bowls with Brown Rice and Smoked Salmon by Jamie Oliver

Time to cook: 40 minutes

Two servings Ingredients:

200g edamame pods, frozen

2 tsp. pickled ginger

smoked salmon (140g)

12 avocados

12 lime juice

12 coriander bunch

12 teaspoon mayonnaise

One teaspoon Sriracha sauce

One teaspoon soy sauce

12 tbsp sesame seeds

twotbsp rice vinegar

One tablespoon mirin

Brown rice, 150g

1. Cook the rice according to package directions, then drain and set aside.

2. Combine the rice wine vinegar, miso, and sesame oil in a mixing bowl.

3. Toss in the rice to moisten it, then drizzle with sesame oil.

4. Combine the mayonnaise, Habanero, lemon zest, and coriander in a small mixing bowl.

5. To serve, divide the rice between two plates.

6. Serve with lemon wedges for drizzling and extra sesame seeds sprinkled on top.

Godzilla Rolls with Shrimp Tempura and Spicy Mayo, 5.8

Time to cook: 13 minutes

One serving size

Ingredients: tempura batter, frying oil

Three tablespoons cream cheese

12 cup all-purpose flour

Rice Sushi

Two avocado slices

1 Nori sheet

To make the Spicy Mayo

2 tbspSriracha chili sauce

One teaspoon sesame oil

12 c. mayonnaise

1. Arrange the bamboo salmon roller mat on a work surface so that the bamboo strips face you vertically.

2. Place the rice on top of the seafood layer.

3. To create the cylinder-shaped sushi, roll the reed mat forward and push the contents inside.

4. Coat the rice roll in cornstarch before dipping it in tempura water and pan-frying it for three minutes, or until the tempura is crisp and lightly browned.

5. In a small mixing bowl, combine the mayonnaise, mustard, and olive oil.

6. Stir until everything is thoroughly combined.

5.9 Grazie

Time to cook: 30 minutes

Ingredients: 1 serving size

cooked rice 150 g

Tamagoyaki 14 of the nori sheet was rolled

12 teaspoon oil

12 teaspoon Shirodashi

12 large eggs

Meatballs with Sweet and Sour Sauce

One teaspoon rice vinegar

1 tsp. katakuriko

One teaspoon sugar

12 tbspmirin 14 cup water

One teaspoon soy sauce

1 tsp. katakuriko

600 mL of oil

12 large eggs

a pinch of sea salt

14 finely chopped onion

250g lean ground pork

5 g of butter

Method:

1. Melt the butter in a small slow cooker.

2. In a mixing bowl, combine the ground beef, egg, salt, cornmeal, and cooked onion.

3. Using your hands, combine everything until it's a little sticky.

4. Shape the meat into 18 ping pong-sized meatballs.

5. Heat the oil to 180°C and pan fry the meatball.

6. In a saucepan, combine the water, torigara soup powders, sesame oil, sugar, mirin, garlic powder, and cornmeal.

7. Simmer it for a few minutes to thicken.

California Crab Rolls 5.10

Time to cook: 35 minutes

36 servings Ingredients:

a dash of wasabi

Six teaspoon soy sauce

1 tbsp toasted sesame seeds

Two teaspoons sushi ginger

Four nori for sushi

Two small crabs, dressed

Sushi rice 500g

12 lemon juice one ripe medium avocado

Four teaspoons sushi vinegar

1. Rinse the rice for up to 30 minutes in warm water, then wash and combine with 850ml water in a medium pot.

2. After peeling and slicing the avocados into long, thin strips, combine them with the lime juice.

3. Sprinkle sesame seeds on the roll before cutting them into 2cm thick slices with a wet knife.

Sushi Cones (5.11 Sushi Cones)

Time to cook: 15 minutes

12 servings Ingredients: 1 large avocado

1 cup cucumber

One teaspoon flakes sea salt

Six toasted nori sheets

12 tbsp rice wine vinegar

One teaspoon caster sugar

a 12 cup sushi rice

112 cup water

12 cup quinoa (white)

1. Bring the quinoa, barley, and milk to a boil in a small saucepan over medium heat.

2. Remove from the heat, cover, and leave to sit for three minutes, or until the potatoes are soft and the liquid has been absorbed.

3. In a small mixing bowl, combine the vinegar, sugar, and salt and stir with a spatula until the glucose and salt are completely dissolved.

4. In a large mixing bowl, combine the grains and millet, then drizzle with the vinegar mixture and fold to combine with a spatula.

5.12 Fukuoka Ramen (Traditional)

Time to cook: 20 minutes

Two servings Ingredients:

One teaspoon dashi

60 mL Soy Sauce, pepper

1 tbsp fish sauce

100 grams cooked pork

100g chicken breast, cooked

20g ginger root, fresh

2 tbsp. sesame seeds

Ramen noodles (300g)

Two green onions

4-gram nori

two eggs

Bamboo shoots (180 g)

80 grams spinach leaves

Method:

1. Cook the pasta until al dente, then drain and rinse under cool water.

2. Immediately plunge the spinach into cold water after one second of blanching.

3. Use a fork to prick the eggshells.

4. Cook the eggs in a pot of boiling water for 5 minutes, or until soft cooked.

5. Remove the eggs from the pan and place them in a bowl of cold water to stop the cooking process.

6. Ladle the scalding hot broth over the assembled soup ingredients in the bowls.

7. Season with pepper to taste.

Chapter 6

Traditional Japanese Vegetarian Recipes

6.1 Donburi with Vegetables

Time to cook: 20 minutes

Four servings Ingredients:

a dozen eggs

Green onion, sliced

1 tbsp. mirin seasoning

One teaspoon caster sugar

One teaspoon miso paste

2 tbsp. light soy sauce

13 cup sushi rice

button mushrooms (150g)

One carrot, large

One broccolini bunch

Method:

1. Cook the rice according to package directions until tender.

2. Cover the food to keep it warm.

2. Pour two tablespoons of cold water into a large, 8cm-deep saucepan.

4. Bring to a simmer over medium-high heat.

5. Broccolini stems, mushrooms, and carrots are optional.

6. Cook, occasionally stirring, for 5 minutes, or until the soft vegetables.

Broccoli florets, miso, sesame oil, mirin spice, and sugar are added to the pan at this point.

8. Pour the egg mixture on top of the vegetables.

9. Cook for 5 minutes, or until the chicken is cooked through.

10. Distribute the rice evenly among the serving dishes.

6.2 Sushi Rice Perfection

Time to cook: 25 minutes

Size of Serving: 15

14 cup white sugar (approximately)

One teaspoon sea salt

a 12 cup risotto vinegar

1 Tbsp. vegetable oil

Three c. water

2 cups uncooked white rice

Method:

1. Wash the grains in a sieve or colander until the water runs clear.

2. Combine the ingredients in a medium saucepan with water.

3. Bring to a simmer, then reduce to low heat and cover for 20 minutes.

4. Allow cooling until you are able to handle it.

5. In a small pot, combine the rice wine vinegar, oil, sugar, and salt.

6. Cook over medium heat until the sugar has dissolved.

7. Allow cooling before adding to the boiled rice.

6.3 Tempura Sweet Potato

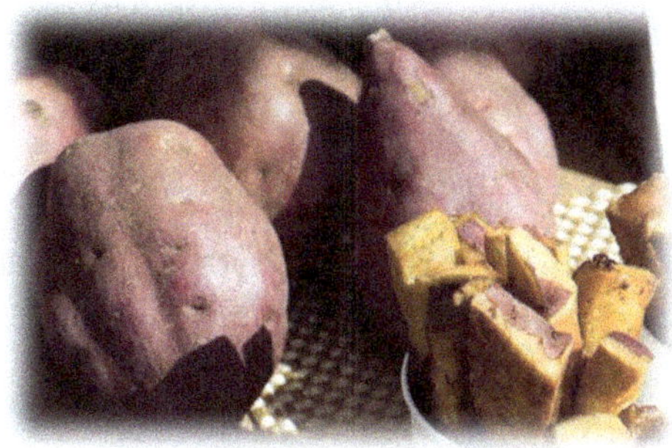

Time to cook: 19 minutes

Four servings Ingredients:

2 cups frying oil

1 pound sweet potato

a quarter cup all-purpose flour

1 tbsp. all-purpose flour

two eggs

a quarter-cup of ice water

3 tbsp of ice water

12 teaspoon of salt

Sauce for dipping

14 tbsp soy sauce

14 oz. rice wine

Method:

1.   Whisk the eggs until foamy in a large mixing bowl. 2. Stir in the salt, 34 cups plus three tablespoons crushed ice, and 34 cups plus one tablespoon wheat just until combined, but the batter remains lumpy.

3. Preheat the oil in a deep or large saucepan to 350°F (175°C).

4. Fry until lightly golden on both sides, about two minutes per side, flipping once.

5. Transfer the cakes to a baking sheet lined with paper towels using a slotted spoon.

6. Repeat with the remaining slices.

6.4 DashiKonbu

Time to cook: 20 minutes

Size of each serving: 4

Ingredients:

2/3 cup kombu

2/3 ozkatsuobushi shaved

2 quarts of ice-cold water

Method:

1. Combine the kombu and liquid in a donabe (clay pot) and immerse the kombu for at least a few minutes.

2. Bring the donation slowly to a boil over a medium flame.

3. Raise the heat to a vigorous simmer and remove it from the heat.

4. All of the katsuobushi should be added at once.

5. Wait until the katsuobushi has settled into the bottom of the donabe.

6. Using a fine-mesh sieve, strain into a bowl.

Soba 6.5 with Toasted Sesame Seed Sauce

Time to cook: 30 minutes

Four servings Ingredients: 5 green onions

3 cups florets broccoli

One garlic clove

One teaspoon sesame oil, dark

12 cup toasted sesame seeds

One teaspoon of white sugar

2 12 tbsp soy sauce

2 tbsp balsamic vinaigrette

Eight oz. soba noodles

Method:

1. Preheat the oven to 375 degrees Fahrenheit (190 degrees Celsius) (190 degrees C).

2. Arrange the spring onions on a rimmed baking sheet.

3. Toast the seeds in a preheated oven for 10 to 15 minutes.

4. Meanwhile, heat a large saucepan of salted water on the stove.

5. Cook for another 6 to 8 minutes, or until the spaghetti is just tender.

6. In a large mixing bowl, combine the wine, honey, sesame oil, garlic, soy sauce, and fresh basil.

7. Toss in the roasted sesame seeds and noodle mixture.

8. After a thorough tossing, add the broccoli.

Tamagoyaki with Mushrooms and Mozzarella Cheese (6.6)

Time to cook: 30 minutes

Size of serving: 2

Ingredients:

twotbsp vegetable oil

1 pound of mozzarella cheese

1 tsp black pepper and 1 tsp salt

14 tsp red chili powder

three eggs

2 12 tbsp. white sugar

Six shiitake mushrooms

Two tablespoons olive oil

Method:

1. Heat the olive oil in a medium saucepan over medium heat.

2. Cook, frequently stirring, for about five minutes, or until the mushrooms have browned and released their liquid.

3. In a mixing bowl, combine the yolks, sugars, pepper, salt, and red chili powder.

4. Cook for 1–2 minutes, or until almost set.

5. Run a heatproof slotted spoon around the edges to loosen them.

6. Arrange the mushrooms on top of the egg, then wrap it up and place it on the skillet's side.

7. Repeat the stacking and rolling procedure with the remaining oil, yolks, onions, and parmesan cheese.

8. Cook the tamagoyaki for 30 seconds on each side, or until they are lightly browned on both sides.

6.7 Nori Vegetarian Rolls

Time to cook: 2 hours

Size of each serving: 5

Ingredients:

12 avocados

One carrot, small

Four sheets of nori seaweed

12 cucumbers

Three oz. firm tofu

Two tablespoons honey

One garlic clove

twotbsp rice vinegar

14 cup water

14 tbsp soy sauce

2 cups uncooked white rice

Method:

1. In a large pot, combine the rice and liquid and set aside for thirty minutes.

2. In a shallow dish, combine the soy sauce, sugar, and ginger.

3. Marinate the tofu for at least a few minutes in this mixture.

4. Bring the water and quinoa to a boil, then reduce to low heat for 20 minutes.

5. Firmly roll the nori from the bottom up, using the mats to help.

6. Repeat with the remaining ingredients.

7. Using a sharp knife, thinly slice into 1-inch slices.

6.8 Freekeh& Vegetables

Cooking Duration: 35 minutes

Size of each serving: 4

Ingredients: Spring Vegetables Salad with Freekeh

14 cup crumbled feta with sea salt and pepper

One bunch radishes broth or water with dill and chives

Two carrots, medium

1 cup fresh English peas

12 teaspoon of salt

1 cup freekeh, cracked

Vinaigrette with Citrus and Dill

12 tsp. sea salt

a few grinds fresh pepper

One shallot, small

One tablespoon dill, fresh

1 tsp. honey, 1 tsp. dijon mustard

14 cup extra virgin olive oil

1 tbsp white wine

14 cup freshly squeezed citrus juice

Method:

1. Combine the freekeh, pepper, and hot water in a small saucepan.

2. Lower the heat to medium and continue to cook until the liquid is absorbed.

3. While the freekeh is cooking, make the dressing.

4. Combine all of the ingredients in a small mixer and blend until smooth.

5. In a mixing bowl, combine the prepared vegetables and cheese.

6. Toss everything together with the Lemon Dill Vinaigrette.

6.9 Pan-Fried Crispy Ramen

Time to cook: 25 minutes

Two servings Ingredients:

One teaspoon soy sauce

One teaspoon rice vinegar

a 12 cup aromatics

Two teaspoons black bean sauce

4 ounces sweet peppers

1 tbsp sesame seed oil

Two eggs from pasture-raised hens

12-pound red cabbage

12 pound fresh ramen noodles

Method:

1. Fill medium saucepan three-quarters full with salted water, cover, and bring to a boil over high heat.

2. Once the water has reached a boil, add the eggs to the saucepan and cook for ten minutes.

3. In a large skillet over medium-high heat, heat the sautéed seasonings until hot. Season with salt and pepper, then add the cabbage and jalapenos.

4. Cook for 5 minutes, or until soft, stirring occasionally. Add the sauce and mix well.

5. Meanwhile, cook the pasta in the same pot of water.

6. Cook for two to three minutes, stirring occasionally, or until the vegetables are tender.

7. Arrange the cooked vegetables and seasoned eggs on top of the finished noodles.

6.10 Ramen with Mushrooms and Bok Choy

1 hour of cooking time

Two servings Ingredients:

One large green onion

Optional salt

Two bokchoy, small

3/4 cup sliced mushrooms

3 cups vegetable broth (low sodium)

One zucchini (medium)

One carrot, medium

12 teaspoon chili garlic sauce

a generous smear of sesame oil

12 tbsp agave nectar 14-inch ginger root

One teaspoon vegetable oil

One garlic clove

threetbsp organic tamari

2 quarts water

14 teaspoon Dijon mustard one pack ramen noodles

1. Fill a medium saucepan halfway with water and bring to a rolling simmer over medium heat.

2. Melt unsalted butter in a small saucepan over low to medium heat.

3. Sauté the mushrooms and green onion whites for a few minutes.

4. Spoon some mushrooms on top with a serving dish.

5. Make your garnishes and arrange them on top of the soup.

Mushroom Mazemen 6.11

Time to cook: 20 minutes

Size of serving: 2

Ingredients:

One tablespoon furikake

14 tsp red pepper flakes

1 tbsp Worcestershire sauce

One teaspoon rice vinegar

One teaspoon soy sauce

Baby bokchoy, 10 oz.

a 12 cup aromatics

One tablespoon brown sugar, light

12 pound fresh ramen noodles

Cremini mushrooms, 4 oz.

Two eggs from pasture-raised hens

1. Fill a medium saucepan halfway with brine, cover, and bring to a boil over high heat. Fresh vegetables should be washed and dried before cooking.

2. Carefully add the eggs to the saucepan of boiling water.

3. Cook for 5 minutes for soft-boiled eggs or until done to taste.

4. Next, in a large medium saucepan, heat one tablespoon of oil until it is hot.

5. Arrange the mushroom pieces in an even layer on top of each other.

6. Cook, without moving, for 3 to 4 minutes, or until lightly browned.

HiyashiChuka (vegetable) 6.12

1 hour of cooking time

Two servings Ingredients:

2 ounces bean sprouts

1 cup arugula

1 tbsp sesame oil

a single tomato

One cucumber (Persian)

One teaspoon sugar

Two eggs from a farm

three scallions

Two teaspoons soy sauce

12 oz freshly made ramen noodles

312 tbsp rice vinegar

One cob of corn

1. Clean and dry fresh vegetables.

2. Bring a medium saucepan of salted water to a boil over high heat.

3. Remove the eggs from the refrigerator and allow them to come to room temperature.

4. In a small mixing bowl, combine honey, olive oil, sesame oil, white tops of onions, leftover rice vinegar, and 12 tablespoons of water.

5. Continue to stir until the sugar has completely dissolved.

6. Set aside while you continue to cook.

7. Once the water begins to boil, add the eggs and cook for 5 minutes.

8. Drain the pasta and divide the sauce among two plates.

On top, you can add corn, lettuce, soft-boiled yolks, tomatoes, bean sprouts, and cucumbers.

Miso Sweet Potato Donburi 6.13

Time to cook: 30 minutes

Two servings Ingredients:

One teaspoon rice vinegar

One tablespoon furikake

14 cup hot sauce

1 tbsp. white miso paste

Two black garlic cloves

One teaspoon mirin

1 pound sushi rice

12-pound cabbage

2 tbsp mayonnaise

1 pound sweet potatoes

two scallions

Two farm eggs from cage-free hens

Method:

1. Preheat the oven to 450°F and place a grill in the center.

2. Season with salt and toss in the sweet potatoes. Toss to coat evenly.

3. Arrange on the rack in an even layer.

4. Roast for 18 to 20 minutes, or until browned and soft when prodded with a fork.

5. Remove the baking sheet from the oven.

6. In a large mixing bowl, combine the chopped cabbage, scallions, sweet chili sauce, and a splash of olive oil; season with salt and pepper to taste.

7. Arrange the roasted potatoes, coleslaw, and soft-boiled eggs on top of the rice. Garnish with Furikake and sliced green scallions tips.

8. Serve with spiced mayonnaise as a garnish.

6.14 Ramen with Spring Peas and Mushrooms

Time to cook: 30 minutes

Two servings Ingredients:

One teaspoon rice vinegar

Two teaspoons black bean sauce

Two tablespoons gochujang

Three tablespoons of soy glaze

One tablespoon kombu

Two eggs from pasture-raised hens

two scallions

4 ounces snow peas

Cremini mushrooms, 4 oz.

12 pound fresh ramen noodles

1. Bring a medium saucepan of salted water to a boil over high heat.

2. While the eggs are cooking, melt two tablespoons of olive butter in a skillet over medium heat.

3. Cook for three to four minutes, or until gently browned and slightly softened, without moving the pan, adding the sliced mushrooms in an even layer.

4. Season with salt and the scallions' cut white tops.

5. Divide the prepared noodles and snow peas between two dishes.

6. Pour in the water and top with the seasoned chicken.

7. Garnish with kombu and the green tips of onions, cut.

6.15 Eggplant with Yakiniku Glaze

Time to cook: 40 minutes

Two servings Ingredients:

One teaspoon sambaloelek

12-pound baby bokchoy

2 tbsp sesame seed oil

One ginger root (1 inch)

212 tbsp yakiniku sauce

2 tspmirin

a single lime

3 tbsp. roasted cashews

two scallions

One ear of corn

shishito peppers, 3 oz

Two garlic cloves

12 cup steamed jasmine rice

Method:

1. Fresh vegetables should be washed and dried before cooking.

2. Peel the ginger and coarsely chop it.

3. Roughly chop the cashews.

4. In the bottom saucepan, combine the rice, a pinch of salt, and 1 cup of water and bring to a boil over medium heat.

5. Before serving, thoroughly mix the juice of two lime wedges into the cooked rice.

6. Divide the cooked rice between two plates.

7. Serve with the cooked vegetables on the side and the sauce on the side.

8. Garnish with green scallions tips and ginger-lime nuts.

6.16 Rice Bowls in Chirashi Style

Time to cook: 50 minutes

Size of serving: 2

Ingredients:

14 sour onion

One small, ripe avocado

12 cup daikon sprigs

12 lemons, medium

1 Persian cucumber, medium

14 cup drained pickled ginger

12 tsp kosher salt

Sushi (8 ounces)

a quarter cup of brown rice

2 tbsp. rice wine vinegar

1 tbsp. brown sugar

12 cup ice-cold water

1. In a small saucepan with a tight-fitting lid, bring flour and lentils to a boil.

2. Reduce heat to a simmer, occasionally stirring, for about 40 minutes, or until water has evaporated and rice is heated through.

3. In a medium bowl, bring the wine, honey, and salt to a boil about 10 to 15 minutes before the rice is done.

4. Take the pan off the heat and whisk in the sugar and salt until completely dissolved.

Summer Soba Salad 6.17

Time to cook: 25 minutes

Size of serving: 3

Ingredients:

Dressing in Sesame, Lime, and Ginger

1.5 teaspoon maple syrup

1 tsp Asian chili sauce

1.5 teaspoon soy sauce

One teaspoon rice vinegar

Lime juice (half a lime)

1 tbsp sesame oil

One tablespoon ginger, minced

Salad with Noodles

Seven spring onions

One cucumber or zucchini

8 ounces Soba Noodles

1 cup carrots, sliced

One small red bell pepper

Method:

1. Combine the dressing ingredients in a mixing bowl.

2. Season with sweetness, spice, and tanginess (lime).

3. Allow for a fifteen-minute chilling period.

4. Cook the pasta according to the package directions.

5. Season with salt or miso if you like it saltier, more sugar if you like it sweeter, and lime or vinegar if you want it tangier.

6.18 Udon Noodle Soup Time to Cook: 10 minutes

Ingredients: 1 serving size

1 tsp salt

1 tsp sugar

One tablespoon soy sauce

One tablespoon mirin

One udon noodle packet

1 tsp. dashi powder

1 cup of hot water

Toppings are optional.

2 tsp. bonito flakes

1 tsp chili powder

One spring onion stalk

Method:

1. If making udon noodles from scratch, follow the package directions or the recipe.

2. Half-fill a deep basin with boiling water, then add the dashi, miso, mirin, salt, and sugar.

3. Toss the cooked udon noodles into the creamy soup.

4. Garnish with sliced spring onions, bonito flakes, and chili flakes.

6.19 Okonomiyaki (Japanese pancakes)

Time to cook: 15 minutes

Two servings Ingredients:

Three beaten eggs

EVOO (extra-virgin olive oil)

1 cup breadcrumbs (panko)

a quarter teaspoon of sea salt

1 14 cup scallions

3 cup packed cabbage

Method:

1. In a large mixing bowl, combine the lettuce, onions, breadcrumbs, and salt.

2. Gently fold the eggs into a small mixing bowl.

3. Preheat a nonstick skillet over medium heat.

4. Spoon the cabbage mixture into the pan using a 14 volumetric flask after brushing it with olive oil.

5. Cook for 3 minutes per side, or until golden brown, lowering the heat as necessary.

6. Drizzle the okonomiyaki with Balsamic vinegar and thin layers of strained mayo.

6.20 Soba Noodles with Seared Tofu

Time to cook: 30 minutes

Four servings Ingredients: cucumber

four radishes

1 tsp red pepper flakes

Four minis or one large

three tbsp. dark brown sugar

One bunch green onions, small

13 cup soy sauce/tamari

One teaspoon ground black pepper

Four cloves garlic

1 (1-inch) ginger piece

2 tbsp sesame seed oil

1 cup soba noodles

2 tbsp canola oil

12-pound firm tofu

Method:

1. Drain the soybeans in a sieve or dry them on a paper towel-lined dish for about 10 minutes while preparing the other ingredients.

2. In the meantime, bring a large pot of water to a boil for the shirataki noodles.

3. Next, cook the soba in hot water for 5 minutes.

4. Add the ginger, onion, and scallion whites to the skillet, along with the remaining tablespoon of sesame oil.

5. In a large mixing bowl, combine the boiled and dried soba noodles, soy sauce, honey, black pepper, bell pepper, and reserved green onions.

Conclusion

Rice is a common ingredient in Japanese cooking. Rice cakes are also popular (mochi). They are available in a variety of flavors and cooking methods, including grilling and boiling. Japanese cuisine has existed for millennia, influenced by both Korea and China. The four seasons and climate are now having a significant impact on Japanese cuisine. The most commonly consumed foods are fish and vegetables.

Although the meal may appear routine to some westerners, the tastiness, presentation, and flavor combination are all important. This book contains a wide range of Japanese meals, including breakfast, snacks, lunch, dinner, soups, and some of the most well-known Japanese recipes. With these recipes, you can start making simple and tasty Japanese dinners.

www.ingramcontent.com/pod-product-compliance
Lightning Source LLC
LaVergne TN
LVHW020607200726
843509LV00001B/12